The Lewis and Clark Expedition

BY
MARIA BACKUS

COPYRIGHT © 2001 Mark Twain Media, Inc.

ISBN 1-58037-180-9

Printing No. CD-1526

Mark Twain Media, Inc., Publishers
Distributed by Carson-Dellosa Publishing Company, Inc.

Table of Contents

About the American History Series

Welcome to *The Lewis and Clark Expedition,* one of the books in the Mark Twain Media, Inc., American History series for students in grades four to seven.

The activity books in this series are designed as stand-alone material for classrooms and home-schoolers or as supplemental material to enhance your history curriculum. Students can be encouraged to use the books as independent study units to improve their understanding of historical events and people.

Each book provides challenging activities that enable students to explore history, geography, and social studies topics. The activities provide research opportunities and promote critical reading, thinking, and writing skills. As students follow the journeys of famous explorers and learn about the people who influenced history, they will draw conclusions; write opinions; compare and contrast historical events, people, and places; analyze cause and effect; and improve mapping skills. Students will also have the opportunity to apply what they learn to their own lives through reflection and creative writing.

Students can further increase their knowledge and understanding of historical events by using reference sources at the library and on the Internet. Students may need assistance to learn how to use search engines and discover appropriate web sites.

Titles of books for additional reading appropriate to the subject matter at this grade level are included in each book.

Although many of the questions are open-ended, answer keys are included at the back of the book for questions with specific answers.

Share a journey through history with your students as you explore the books in the Mark Twain Media, Inc., American History series:

Discovering and Exploring the Americas
Life in the Colonies
The American Revolution
The Lewis and Clark Expedition
The Westward Movement
The California Gold Rush
The Oregon and Santa Fe Trails
Slavery in the United States
The American Civil War
Abraham Lincoln and His Times
The Reconstruction Era
Industrialization in America
The Roaring Twenties and Great Depression
World War II and the Post-War Years
America in the 1960s and 1970s
America in the 1980s and 1990s

Time Line

1770 William Clark is born in Virginia.

1774 Meriwether Lewis is born in Virginia.

1801 Lewis becomes President Jefferson's personal secretary.

1803 The United States purchases the Louisiana Territory.

1804 May 14   The expedition leaves St. Louis.

August 20   Sergeant Floyd dies of appendicitis near Sioux City, Iowa.

October 25   The expedition reaches the Mandan villages. They build Fort Mandan and stay for the winter.

1805 April 7   They leave Fort Mandan and travel west on the Missouri River.

June 13   Lewis arrives at Great Falls on the Missouri River.

June 22   They begin the portage around Great Falls.

July 4   They complete the portage around Great Falls.

July 25   The expedition arrives at Three Forks on the Missouri River.

September   The expedition crosses the Rocky Mountains.

November   They build Fort Clatsop near the Pacific Ocean and stay for the winter.

1806 March 23   The expedition leaves Fort Clatsop and heads home.

September 21   They arrive back in St. Louis.

1807 Lewis becomes the Governor of the Louisiana Territory.

Clark becomes the Superintendent of Indian Affairs for the Louisiana Territory.

Name: _____ Date: _____

Meet Meriwether Lewis

Read about Meriwether Lewis's early years, and fill in the cause-and-effect chart below.

Meriwether Lewis was born on a plantation near Charlottesville, Virginia, on August 18, 1774. When the American War of Independence began in 1775, his father, John Lewis, left home to fight against the British. His father died of pneumonia in 1779 while on leave from the war. His mother remarried a short time later, and the family moved to Georgia after the war.

There were no schools in Georgia in 1779, so Lewis had time to hunt, fish, and roam the woods. He became an excellent woodsman. Because he was interested in the plants in the area, his mother taught him how to make herbal medicines.

Lewis returned to Virginia when he was thirteen to attend school. He also learned to manage the family's plantation that had been left to him.

By 1794, Lewis was ready for a change. When President George Washington asked for volunteers to help put down the Whiskey Rebellion, Lewis joined the Virginia militia. He enjoyed his experience in the militia, so he decided to join the regular army. He was then assigned to the rifle company in Fort Greenville, Ohio. It was there that he met and became a friend of Captain William Clark.

Cause	Effect
1. The American War of Independence began in 1775.	1. _____
2. _____	2. Lewis had time to hunt, fish, and roam the woods.
3. _____	3. Lewis learned how to make medicines.
4. Lewis returned to Virginia.	4. _____
5. _____	5. Lewis joined the regular army.
6. Lewis was assigned to the rifle company in Fort Greenville, Ohio.	6. _____

Name: _____ Date: _____

Meet William Clark

Read the paragraphs about William Clark's early years. Fill in the summary chart below.

William Clark was born near Richmond, Virginia, on August 1, 1770. All five of his older brothers fought against the British in the American War of Independence. When Clark was fourteen, his family moved to the western frontier. This is now present-day Kentucky. There were no schools there, so his older brothers helped him learn natural history and science.

At that time, forests covered Kentucky. Because Clark spent much of his time roaming the woods, he became highly skilled in hunting, fishing, tracking, camping, and land navigation.

Kentucky was also home to the Shawnee and Wabash tribes. Clark joined his older brother George to fight the natives who were understandably upset that the white settlers were taking their land from them.

In 1789, Clark became a soldier and was eventually promoted to the rank of captain. While in the army, Clark learned to understand and respect the Native Americans. It was while he was commanding a rifle company in Ohio that Captain Clark met and became friends with Meriwether Lewis.

1. **Birth**

   Date: _____

   Place: _____

2. **Family Move**

   From: _____

   To: _____

3. **Education**

   Studied: _____

   _____

   _____

   _____

4. **Outdoor Skills**

   _____

   _____

   _____

   _____

5. **Military Service**

   Rank: _____

   _____

6. **Relationship With Native Americans**

   _____

   _____

Name: _____ Date: _____

Important Words to Learn

Use a dictionary to define each of the following words. Draw a picture to illustrate each word.

1. Botany _____

   _____

   _____

2. Zoology _____

   _____

   _____

3. Naturalist _____

   _____

   _____

4. Herb _____

   _____

   _____

5. Celestial _____

   _____

   _____

6. Navigate _____

   _____

   _____

7. Expedition _____

   _____

   _____

Name: _____ Date: _____

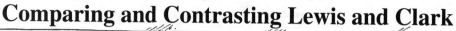

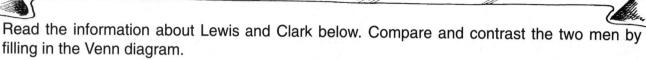
Comparing and Contrasting Lewis and Clark

Read the information about Lewis and Clark below. Compare and contrast the two men by filling in the Venn diagram.

Meriwether Lewis was born in Virginia. He had five years of formal schooling. He also learned to hunt, fish, and make herbal medicines. He was an excellent amateur naturalist. Before the expedition started, he studied medicine, botany, zoology, and celestial navigation. He was over six feet tall, had a slender build, and had dark hair. He was often moody and impatient. He preferred to be by himself rather than with other people. He had been a captain in the army.

William Clark was born in Virginia. Although he did not have much formal schooling, his older brothers helped him with his studies. He became an experienced geographer, mapmaker, nature artist, and riverboatman. He had excellent hunting, fishing, trapping, and camping skills. He was over six feet tall, had a stocky build, and had bright red hair. He was sociable and even-tempered. He had been a captain in the army.

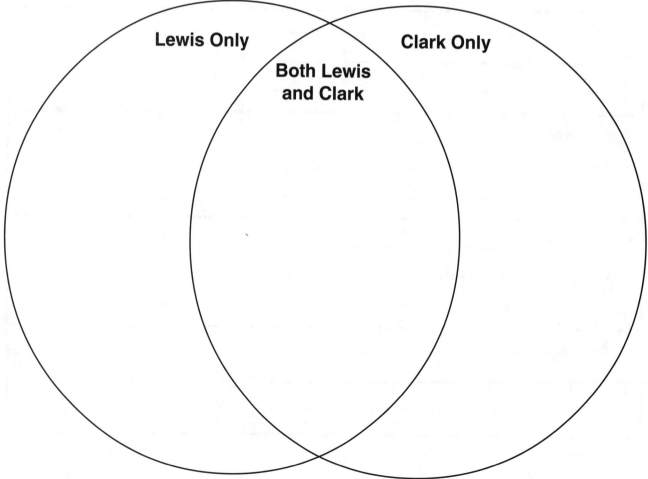

Lewis Only

Both Lewis and Clark

Clark Only

Name: _____   Date: _____

Thomas Jefferson's Dream

Read the paragraphs about what Thomas Jefferson wanted to accomplish. Complete the mapping activity below.

When Thomas Jefferson became the third President of the United States in 1801, he needed someone to become his personal secretary. Jefferson had known the Lewis family for a long time because they had been neighbors in Virginia. He decided to ask Meriwether Lewis to be his new secretary, and Lewis was pleased to accept the job.

At this time, the land to the west of the Mississippi River was largely unknown. Some white settlers called this land the Great Unknown or the Back of Beyond.

President Jefferson asked Lewis to lead an expedition through this land. What Jefferson wanted Lewis to find most of all was a water route from the Missouri River leading west to the Pacific Ocean. A water route would make it much easier to trade with China and other lands in the Far East. The only other way ships could trade with China was to sail all the way around South America and cross the Pacific Ocean, and then the ships had to travel back again. This voyage would last from two to three years!

1. Look at the map at the right. Show the route a trading ship would take from the port of New Orleans to China and back. Use an atlas to help you label the Atlantic Ocean, the Gulf of Mexico, the Pacific Ocean, North America, Central America, and South America.

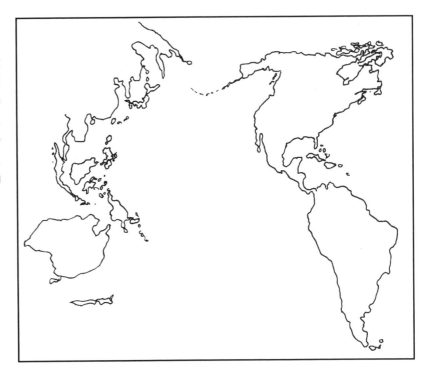

2. What would be the advantage of a river route across America to the Pacific Ocean?

_____

_____

Name: _____ Date: _____

The Louisiana Purchase

Read the paragraphs about the Louisiana Purchase and complete the mapping activity below.

The land that President Jefferson wanted Lewis to explore did not belong to the United States. Although the land was the home of many Native Americans, Spain claimed this land as its own. It was known as the Louisiana Territory. For a time, Jefferson and Lewis kept their plans a secret. They did not want the Spanish to know that they were planning an expedition into Spanish territory.

Then, Napoleon Bonaparte of France forced Spain to give the Louisiana Territory to France in a secret treaty. Bonaparte, however, needed money for his war against Great Britain. He agreed to sell the entire Louisiana Territory to the United States for 15 million dollars. The Louisiana Purchase doubled the size of the United States. The purchase was also a great opportunity for President Jefferson— now the expedition would travel at least partly through American territory instead of Spanish territory.

1. The map below shows the Louisiana Territory. Use an atlas to determine which 15 modern states were at least partially formed from the Louisiana Purchase.

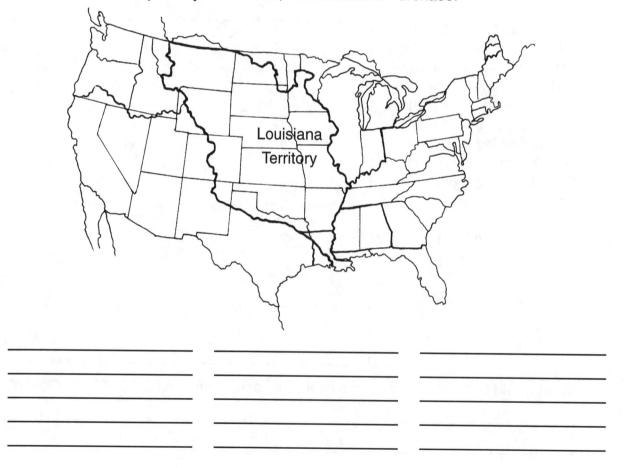

_____   _____   _____

_____   _____   _____

_____   _____   _____

_____   _____   _____

8

Name: _____ Date: _____

The Oregon Country

Read the paragraph about the Oregon Country and answer the questions below.

　　The mountainous region beyond the Louisiana Territory was known as the Oregon Country. This land was the home of many Native Americans. Spain, Russia, and Great Britain all wanted a share of this area. President Jefferson also wanted this land for the United States. He thought he would be able to negotiate with the Native Americans after the expedition was over. He believed they could be persuaded to give up their land and their way of life. He thought they would not mind living among the white settlers as farmers.

1.　Which four states were formed from the Oregon Country?

_____

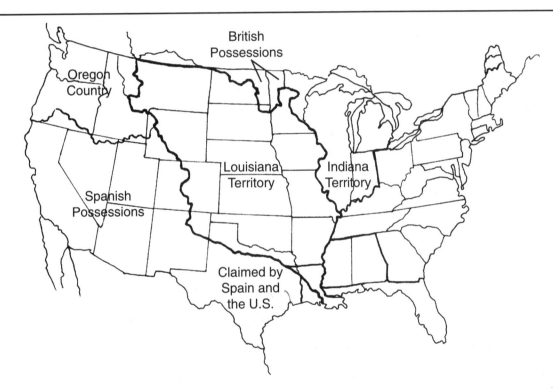

2.　What do you think about President Jefferson's idea that the Native Americans could be persuaded to give up their land and their way of life to become farmers? Write a paragraph explaining your ideas.

_____

_____

_____

_____

_____

Name: _____ Date: _____

A Letter to William Clark

Read the paragraphs below about Lewis's decision to invite William Clark to be a co-commander of the expedition.

President Jefferson wanted Lewis to do more than find a river route to the Pacific Ocean. He wanted him to draw accurate maps that included important landmarks and campsites, as well as latitude and longitude markings. Jefferson also wanted Lewis to record information about the climate, soil, plants, and animals. In addition, he told him to make friends with the Native Americans and to find out about their languages, houses, religions, appearance, laws, and customs. He wanted to know what items they would like to trade or buy from the United States. He also wanted Lewis to keep a detailed journal of what happened on the expedition.

Lewis thought the expedition would have a better chance of success if it had a second leader. He decided to ask his friend William Clark to join him as a co-commander. At that time, Clark had returned to his family's plantation in Kentucky.

1. Imagine that you are Lewis. Write a letter to your good friend William Clark telling him all about the expedition. Explain the mission to him in detail. Next, request that he join you as a co-commander. Tell why you think he would make an excellent leader. Use reference books and information from the previous pages.

June 19, 1803

Dear William,

_____

_____

_____

_____

_____

_____

_____

_____

_____

_____

_____

Sincerely,
Meriwether Lewis

Name: _____ Date: _____

Preparing for a Journey

Read the preparations Lewis made for his journey. Next, think about the types of journeys you have made. Perhaps you have moved to another city or state. Perhaps you have hiked through the mountains or vacationed with your family. Finally, write about the preparations you made for your journey.

Lewis had many tasks to do before he set out on the expedition. Some of these tasks included:

- Deciding the amount and kinds of supplies that would be needed
- Overseeing the construction of a custom keelboat
- Gathering medical supplies and scientific equipment
- Studying medicine, botany, zoology, and celestial observation
- Finding and buying supplies, including items for trade with Native Americans
- Recruiting crew members

1. What kind of preparations did you make for your journey?

_____

_____

2. What kind of preparations did your parents need to make?

_____

_____

3. How did your preparations make your journey proceed more smoothly?

_____

_____

4. What could you have done to make your journey even more enjoyable or successful?

_____

_____

5. Write a paragraph on your own paper describing your journey. Note the preparations you made or should have made. Explain how your preparations (or your lack of preparations) affected your journey.

Name: _____ Date: _____

Getting Your Bearings

To prepare for the trip, Lewis spent time with Andrew Ellicott, an astronomer, and Robert Patterson, a professor of mathematics. Patterson gave Lewis a formula to help him compute longitude through observations of the moon.

Use a dictionary to write a definition for the following words:

1. Latitude _____

_____

2. Longitude _____

_____

3. Sextant _____

_____

4. Octant _____

_____

Use an atlas to find the approximate latitude and longitude of each of the following places:

5. Philadelphia, Pennsylvania _____

6. Louisville, Kentucky _____

7. St. Louis, Missouri _____

8. Bismarck, North Dakota _____

9. Council Bluffs, Iowa _____

10. Astoria, Oregon _____

Name: _____ Date: _____

Lining up the Crew

After many delays, Lewis finally left Pittsburgh on August 31, 1803. His first task was to take his newly-built keelboat down the Ohio River to Louisville, Kentucky. The trip was slow because the river was low and full of sandbars. Sometimes he and the soldiers who were with him had to unload the boat and lift it over the sand and rocks. They didn't reach Louisville until October 15, 1803.

Lewis met Clark and his black slave, York, along with several volunteers in Louisville. As they continued down the Ohio River, they stopped at army posts and asked the commanders for men who might be suitable for the expedition.

1. Imagine that you are Captain Lewis. You need men with a variety of skills, talents, and personality traits for a long, dangerous expedition into an unknown land. You decide to put up a note at each army post explaining your need for crew members for what you now call the "Corps of Discovery." Write your note below. Describe the specific types of skills, talents, and personality traits you are looking for.

WANTED
Hardworking Men for the Corps of Discovery

_____

_____

_____

_____

_____

_____

_____

_____

Name: _____   Date: _____

Applying for the Corps of Discovery

1. You have decided to apply for the Corps of Discovery. Write a letter to Captain Lewis explaining why you think you would make a good crew member. Describe your specific skills or talents. For example, you may be good at handling a boat; drawing maps; observing, describing, or drawing plants and animals; communicating with the Native Americans; problem-solving; mediating conflicts; cooking; hunting; fishing; or journal writing. Also, explain why your personality traits would benefit the expedition.

October 30, 1803

Dear Captain Lewis,

_____

_____

_____

_____

_____

_____

_____

_____

_____

_____

Sincerely,

Name: _____   Date: _____

Planning the Supplies

1. It is the year 1804, and you are now a member of the Corps of Discovery. It is your job to determine which supplies to take on the expedition. There are more than thirty men traveling with you. You will be gone for more than a year. You will need to take medical items, navigational equipment, food, utensils, clothing, as well as hunting and fishing supplies. Work with a partner. Discuss the types of items you would need and that were available in 1804. List the items below.

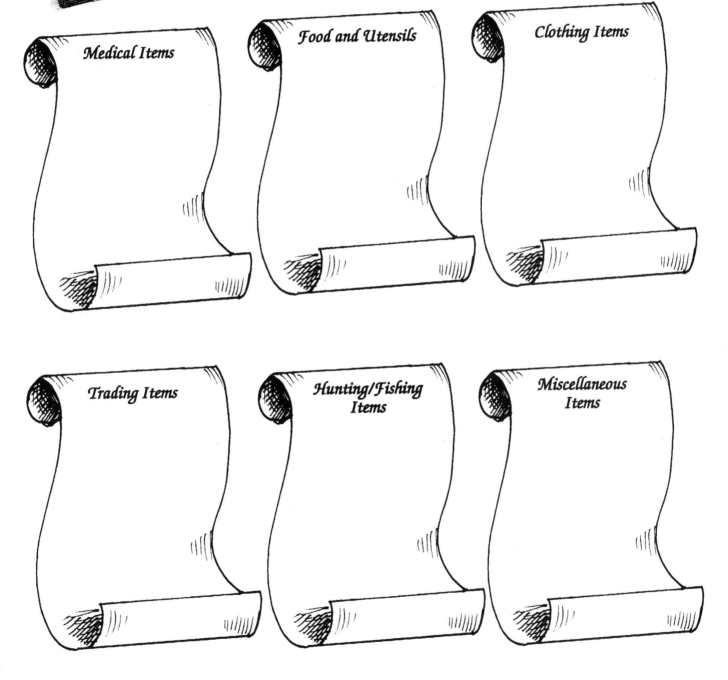

Medical Items

Food and Utensils

Clothing Items

Trading Items

Hunting/Fishing Items

Miscellaneous Items

Name: _____ Date: _____

The Actual Supplies

Read the partial list of supplies that Lewis and Clark took on the expedition and answer the questions below.

List of Supplies

1 mariner's compass	6 copper kettles
4 tin blowing trumpets	12 gross fishing hooks
24 iron spoons	2 pick axes
1 microscope	rope
1 tape measure	nails
6 papers of ink powder	spades
4 metal pens	vises
15 rifles	portable soup
1 pound of ointment for blisters	dried and salted rations
2 crayons	mosquito curtains
1 pair of pocket pistols	medicine
30 linen shirts	scientific & mathematical equipment
blankets, coats, socks	knives
air gun	books about plants and animals
cannons for the boats	blacksmith tools

1. Which items did you *not* expect to see on the above list? Explain why.

   _____

   _____

2. Which items do you think would be important to take that are not on the above list? Explain why.

   _____

   _____

3. What kinds of items would you take on an expedition today that were not available in 1804?

   _____

   _____

Name: _____ Date: _____

The Trade Goods

1. Read the list of items that Lewis and Clark took to trade with the Native Americans. Next, think about the Native Americans' point of view in 1804. Which items would be the most useful to them? Which items were decorative? Which kinds of items might they have already obtained from fur traders? Work with a partner to fill in the charts below. You may put an item in more than one category.

Items for Trade

red silk handkerchiefs	eyeglasses
copper wire	glass beads
ribbons	tinsel tassels
brass buttons	burning glasses
fish hooks	small paper bells
jewelry	silver peace medals
blankets	knives
calico shirts	kettles
needles, thread, scissors, thimbles	hatchets
mirrors	tobacco

Useful Items

_____
_____
_____
_____
_____
_____
_____
_____

Decorative Items

_____
_____
_____
_____
_____
_____
_____
_____

Items Possibly Obtained from Fur Traders

_____
_____
_____
_____
_____
_____
_____
_____

Name: _____ Date: _____

Problems and Solutions

Read each paragraph below. Identify the problem and the solution in each paragraph.

1. Captains Lewis and Clark continued their journey down the Ohio River. They reached the Mississippi River in November of 1803. From there, they traveled up the Mississippi River to the Missouri River. It was too late to continue on their expedition because the Missouri River froze in winter. The men built Camp Wood across from the mouth of the Missouri River, about 20 miles north of St. Louis. They stayed there until spring.

   Problem: _____

   Solution: _____

2. There were more than 45 men at Camp Wood during that winter. Some of them had been soldiers, but many of them were civilians. Many of them did not know how to shoot a rifle correctly. Captain Clark made them undergo constant rifle practice.

   Problem: _____

   Solution: _____

3. The men trained and drilled all winter. Some of the men became unruly. They fought with each other and refused to follow orders. In March, the captains dismissed those men who didn't qualify. Twenty-six men were chosen for the permanent party—those who would go to the Pacific coast.

   Problem: _____

   Solution: _____

4. President Jefferson wanted to be informed of the expedition's progress along the way. The captains chose a small number of soldiers to come with the expedition for a while. Then they would take the keelboat filled with reports and artifacts back to St. Louis for President Jefferson.

   Problem: _____

   Solution: _____

5. Look in a reference book. Find one other problem that happened to the expedition *before* they even got underway. Write the problem and solution on another sheet of paper.

Name: _____ Date: _____

Reviewing the Journey: Part 1

The paragraph below reviews the route Lewis followed from Pittsburgh to St. Louis. Read the paragraph and do the mapping activity below.

Lewis and the soldiers had traveled on the empty keelboat southwest on the Ohio River from Pittsburgh, Pennsylvania, to Louisville, Kentucky. There they had met Clark and continued down the Ohio River to the Mississippi River. From there they had traveled up the Mississippi River to the Missouri River. They stopped for the winter and built Camp Wood, which was twenty miles north of St. Louis.

1. Use reference books to label the following rivers and states:
    • Ohio River, Mississippi River, Missouri River
    • Pennsylvania, Ohio, West Virginia, Kentucky, Indiana, Illinois, Missouri

2. Use a dot to indicate the location of these cities:
    • Pittsburgh, Pennsylvania; Louisville, Kentucky; and St. Louis, Missouri

3. Use a red pencil to indicate the route Lewis followed from Pittsburgh to St. Louis.

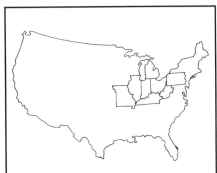

Name: _____ Date: _____

Meet the Crew

Read the information about each person below. Choose the person who seems most interesting to you. Write a paragraph on another sheet of paper from that person's point of view. Describe the person's thoughts and feelings the day before the expedition starts. Tell what last minute preparations the person is making for the trip. Use the words "I," "me," or "mine" to help you write from the person's point of view.

GEORGE DROUILLARD
Translator; fluent in Native American sign language; excellent hunter and woodsman

JOHN SHIELDS
Age 35—Oldest member of expedition; married; gunsmith; blacksmith

YORK
Clark's slave; expedition cook

JOHN ORDWAY
Top sergeant at Camp Wood; ordered to keep a journal

PIERRE CRUZATTE
River navigator; fiddler

SEAMAN
Lewis's Newfoundland dog; catches squirrels; guards camp

Name: _____ Date: _____

The Keelboat and the Pirogues

Read the paragraph and answer the questions below.

On a rainy Monday, May 14, 1804, the expedition officially got underway. Lewis was still in St. Louis and planned to join the men later at St. Charles, 20 miles up the Missouri River. According to Clark, the men were in high spirits as they rowed the three boats away from Camp Wood. The first boat was the keelboat that had been custom built for the expedition. The other two boats were called pirogues. The men were not used to handling the heavy boats, which all together were packed with about 21,000 pounds of supplies! They were only able to travel four miles on the first day.

1. Use a dictionary to define *keelboat* and *pirogue.* _____

    _____

2. From which language is the word *pirogue* directly taken? _____

3. Use reference books or the Internet to find more information and a picture of the keelboat and the pirogues. Do *one* of the following assignments in the space below.

    A. Draw a picture of the men in the keelboat and the two pirogues getting underway on the Missouri River. Use accurate details including the correct number of oars on each boat and the colors of the boats. Indicate the dimensions of the keelboat.

    B. Imagine that you are spectator watching the boats leave from Camp Wood. Write a paragraph that captures the spirit of the moment. Describe what you see, hear, touch, smell, and taste.

Name: _____ Date: _____

The Muddy Missouri

Read each question below, then fill in the box labeled "My Ideas."

1. According to folklore, the Missouri River was part water and part mud and sand. Out of ten parts, how many parts do you think would be water? How many parts would be mud and sand?

My Ideas	Actual Information

2. List two ways the men could get the boats around sandbars.

My Ideas	Actual Information

3. What other problems might the river present?

My Ideas	Actual Information

4. About how many miles do you think the boats would travel in a typical day?

My Ideas	Actual Information

Read the paragraph below, then go back and fill in the boxes labeled "Actual Information."

According to folklore, the Missouri River was made up of four parts water and six parts sand and mud. It was even called the "Big Muddy." The river was filled with snags and sandbars that could tear holes in the boats. There were also stretches of hazardous boulders and rapids. The men could sometimes hoist a sail, but usually they rowed or poled the boats upstream against the current. Sometimes, the men had to slog along the muddy shore and pull the heavy boats using cordelles, or towropes. They traveled only about 12 to 14 miles a day.

22

Name: _____ Date: _____

Daily Life on the Missouri

What was the daily routine like on the Missouri River? Read the information below to find out, then do *one* of the activities in the space below.

The men were up at sunrise and on the river by 7:00 A.M. Captain Clark was the better riverboatman, so he usually stayed on the keelboat drawing maps and supervising the men. Captain Lewis was the better naturalist, so he usually walked along the shore or rode one of their two horses. He investigated the plants, animals, soil, and minerals.

There were three sergeants on board the keelboat who looked for Native Americans, watched for obstacles in the river, reported islands and streams to the captain, and kept the men working.

It was hard work for the privates who had to row, pole, or tow the boats against the current. George Drouillard and John Shields spent each day hunting for deer or other game. They hung their quarry from high trees along the river for the men to find. In the afternoon, scouts looked ahead for a good campsite. In the evening, the men secured the boats, gathered firewood, and pitched their tents. York gathered salad greens and cooked their supper. Some men were on guard duty each night. If the men weren't too tired, they wrote in journals or danced and sang as Pierre Cruzatte played the fiddle.

1. Draw a *detailed, colorful* picture showing a scene from the Corps of Discovery's daily life on the Missouri. For example, you could draw a picture of Captain Lewis walking along the shore with his horse or examining plants. You could draw a picture of the men dancing as Pierre Cruzatte played the violin.

2. Write a paragraph of at least five sentences explaining which job you would have liked to do. Explain why you would have been good at that job.

Name: _____ Date: _____

The Great Plains

Read the paragraphs about some of the animals that the expedition encountered. Choose one of the animals. Use reference books to find out more about the animal. On the journal page below, write a short description of this animal. Make a sketch of the animal next to your description.

The Corps of Discovery continued to travel west on the Missouri River. When they arrived at the place where Kansas City, Missouri, now stands, the river made a great bend to the north. Beyond this area, the men first saw the Great Plains. Clark wrote in his journal about the grass, springs, brooks, shrubs covered in delicious fruit, and the scented flowers. The Great Plains teemed with wildlife. There were beavers in the streams and elk and deer in the woods. Buffalo herds roamed the plains.

Many of the animals were new to the members of the expedition. They had never before seen a badger, coyote, pronghorn, jackrabbit, mule deer, bull snake, or a magpie. Clark drew sketches of the animals, and Lewis described each one in his journal. They collected and preserved samples of plants and animals to send back to President Jefferson.

My Sketch

Name: _____ Date: _____

Les Petits Chiens

One animal that the men had never seen before was a prairie dog. The Frenchmen in the Corps of Discovery called these creatures *les petits chiens,* which means "the little dogs." Captain Lewis was determined to capture a live prairie dog and have it sent to President Jefferson. The men had quite a time figuring out how to do this.

1. Use reference books to find out more about prairie dogs. Write a short description on the journal page below. Answer the following questions:

   How big are prairie dogs?
   What do they look like?
   How do they communicate with each other?
   How long are their tunnels under the ground?
   Why is it difficult to catch one?
   How did the men finally catch one?

2. Draw a picture of a prairie dog next to the description.

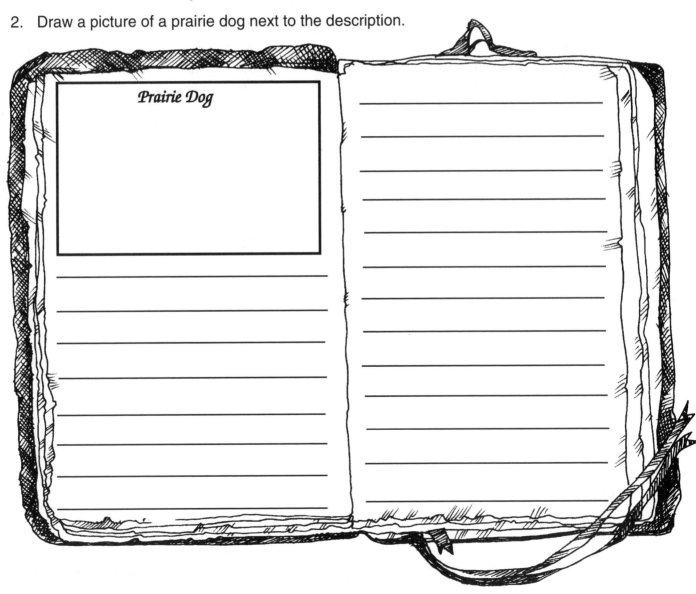

Prairie Dog

Name: _____   Date: _____

The First Council With the Native Americans

Read the paragraphs about what Lewis and Clark wanted from the Native Americans and what the Native Americans wanted from the expedition. Fill in the charts below.

The Corps of Discovery continued north on the Missouri River. By July 21, 1804, they passed the mouth of the Platte River. They were now in the territory of the Oto and Missouri tribes. It was summer, and most of the Native Americans had gone west to hunt buffalo. Lewis and Clark finally arranged to meet several minor chiefs for a council near present-day Council Bluffs, Iowa.

Lewis and Clark made the council as ceremonious as possible. The captains dressed in uniforms and paraded their men. They hoisted the American flag, exchanged gifts with the Native Americans, and smoked a ceremonial native pipe. Lewis and Clark told them that President Jefferson was now their "Great Father" and that their land was now governed by the United States instead of France. They wanted the Native Americans to live in peace with other tribes. They also wanted them to trade only with the United States.

The Native Americans told Lewis and Clark that they needed to protect themselves from other tribes, especially from the better-armed Teton Sioux who were becoming very powerful in the area. The Native Americans wanted to trade with anyone—Spanish, British, French, the expedition—who would give them better ways to wage war.

What Lewis and Clark wanted from the Native Americans	**What the Native Americans wanted from the expedition**
_____	_____
_____	_____
_____	_____
_____	_____
_____	_____
_____	_____

Why do you think that neither side got what it wanted? _____

_____

_____

26

Name: _____ Date: _____

Now and Then

What do you and the Corps of Discovery have in common? Look at the items below. Decide whether each item is something *only* the men on the expedition might have done, *only* something that people today might do, or something that the men did then *and* people do today. Put an X in the appropriate columns.

	Crew	People today	Both
1. Go for a swim			
2. Dance, sing, listen to music			
3. Watch a movie			
4. Play checkers			
5. Observe plants and animals			
6. Read a book			
7. Write letters			
8. Take a nature walk			
9. Trade blacksmith services for corn			
10. Swat mosquitoes			
11. Hunt buffalo			
12. Converse in sign language			
13. Row a keelboat			
14. Use a computer			
15. Write in a journal			
16. Gather berries			
17. Play baseball			
18. Eat soup			

Name: _____ Date: _____

The Teton Sioux

Read the paragraphs and note the order in which events happened.

The Teton Sioux lived on both sides of the Missouri River in what is now South Dakota. They tried to control any trade between fur traders from St. Louis and other tribes that lived upstream. The Teton Sioux would allow fur traders to pass only after they had given the Sioux enough gifts.

The first group of Sioux arrived at the Corps of Discovery's camp in late September of 1804. They were not impressed by the corps' uniforms or by the air gun. They seized one of the expedition's pirogues and all its cargo. The situation became tense as the Sioux readied their bows with arrows, and the crew aimed their rifles. Then the chief, Black Buffalo, decided to return the pirogue and ask for peace.

The expedition still hoped to become friends with the Sioux, so they visited the Sioux village where there were about eighty tepees. There they ate dog meat and pemmican. The Sioux men and women performed dances for the explorers, but the situation remained tense. That night, the men moved their boats a mile up the river from the Sioux village. For the next three days, more Sioux began to arrive at the village. Finally, Black Buffalo allowed Lewis and Clark to leave in exchange for some tobacco.

The Lewis and Clark expedition did not succeed in making friends with the Sioux; however, both sides avoided any bloodshed, and the expedition continued up the Missouri River.

Number the events below in the order in which they occurred.

_____ A. The Sioux seized one of the expedition's pirogues.

_____ B. Black Buffalo allowed Lewis and Clark to leave after they gave him some tobacco.

_____ C. The Sioux forced fur traders to give them gifts before they could continue upriver.

_____ D. The Sioux were not impressed by the corps' uniforms or by the air gun.

_____ E. The expedition first met the Sioux in late September of 1804.

_____ F. Black Buffalo returned the pirogue.

_____ G. For three days, more and more Sioux arrived at the village.

_____ H. The Sioux readied their bows; the corps aimed their rifles.

_____ I. The expedition visited the Sioux village.

_____ J. The men moved their boats a mile up the river from the Sioux village.

Name: _____ Date: _____

Winter at Fort Mandan

Read the paragraphs below. Use the information to compare and contrast how the men and the Native Americans spent the winter at Fort Mandan. Fill in the charts below.

By October 1804, the expedition had traveled 1,600 miles from St. Louis up the Missouri River to the Mandan Villages in what is now western North Dakota. The Mandans did not mind if the Corps wintered near them. The men built a small fort and named it Fort Mandan in honor of the Mandans.

The winter was bitterly cold. The men struggled to stay warm while the Mandans, wearing very few clothes, often played lacrosse on the frozen river. The men set up a blacksmith shop where they sharpened and repaired axes, hoes, and other metal tools for the Mandans. The Mandans paid them with corn for this service. During the winter, both the men and the Mandans hunted together for buffalo. Almost every day, the Mandans or the Hidatsa, a neighboring tribe, visited the fort. They examined the keelboat and the blacksmith shop. They also were curious about York, since they had never seen a person of African-American heritage before. On New Year's Day, 16 men visited the Mandan Village and danced for the Mandans. Lewis and Clark spent the winter writing detailed reports and making accurate maps for President Jefferson.

How the Mandans Spent the Winter

_____
_____
_____
_____
_____
_____
_____
_____
_____

How the Corps Spent the Winter

_____
_____
_____
_____
_____
_____
_____
_____
_____

Name: _____ Date: _____

Reviewing the Journey: Part 2

The paragraph below reviews the route the Corps of Discovery followed. Read the paragraph, then do the mapping activity below.

The Corps of Discovery had traveled west on the Missouri River from St. Louis. The river turned to the north where present-day Kansas City, Missouri, now stands. By July 21, the men had gone almost 600 miles and passed the mouth of the Platte River. The Corps continued north on the Missouri River. Lewis and Clark held their first council with the Oto near Council Bluffs, Iowa. Sergeant Charles Floyd died of appendicitis near present-day Sioux City, Iowa. They had an unfriendly encounter with the Teton Sioux in South Dakota, and then continued north to the Mandan villages near what is now Bismarck, North Dakota.

1. Use reference books to label the following rivers, states, and cities on the map below:
   • Missouri River, Platte River
   • Missouri, Kansas, Nebraska, Iowa, South Dakota, North Dakota
   • St. Louis and Kansas City in Missouri; Council Bluffs and Sioux City in Iowa; and Bismarck in North Dakota

2. Use a red pencil to indicate the route the expedition took from St. Louis to the Mandan villages.

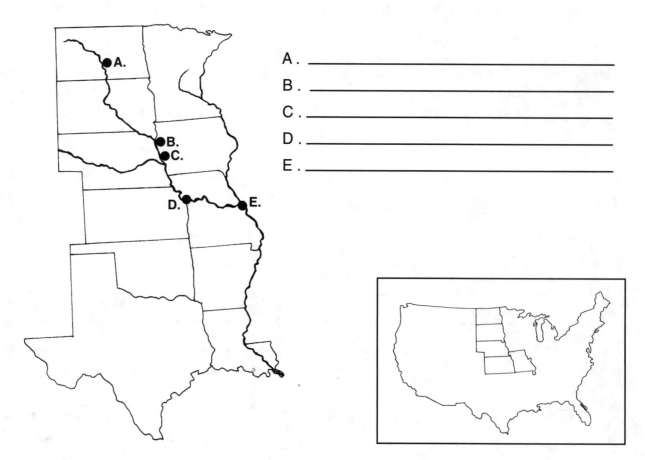

A. _____

B. _____

C. _____

D. _____

E. _____

Name: _____   Date: _____

In Mathematical Terms

Read each story problem and answer the question.

1. Lewis was born in August of 1774, and Clark was born in August of 1770. Which man was older? How much older was he? _____

2. The American War of Independence began in 1775. Why didn't Lewis or Clark take part in the war? _____

3. The Lewis and Clark expedition began in May of 1804. How old was Lewis at that time? How old was Clark? Hint: Note their birth dates. _____

4. The youngest man in the Corps of Discovery was 18 years old and the oldest man was 35 years old. How many years apart were these two men in age? _____

5. The Lewis and Clark expedition passed the mouth of the Platte River about 600 miles from St. Louis. By the time they had reached the Mandan villages in North Dakota, they had traveled a total of 1,600 miles. How far had they traveled beyond the mouth of the Platte River to the Mandan Villages? _____

6. The keelboat and the two pirogues left St. Louis carrying almost 21,000 pounds of cargo. If the cargo had been divided equally among the three boats, how many pounds of cargo would each boat carry? _____

7. The privates received $280 for their work. They worked for 28 months. How much did they receive per month? _____

8. The privates actually received double the usual amount because of their good work. How much would privates ordinarily be paid per month? _____

9. If each tepee in the Teton Sioux village was made up of 25 buffalo hides sewn together and draped over a frame of long poles, how many buffalo hides would be needed for 80 tepees? _____

10. According to some reports, Sacajawea died in 1812. According to other reports, she died in 1884. How many more years would she have lived if she died in 1884 instead of in 1812? _____

Name: _____   Date: _____

From One Language to Another

Read the paragraphs about the difficulties of translating from one language to another. Complete the activities below.

Lewis and Clark wanted to learn all they could about the land west of Fort Mandan. They knew that the Hidatsa had sent war parties west toward the Rockies to raid the Shoshone. The captains asked the Hidatsa about the land to the west of Fort Mandan.

It was hard work to translate from English to Hidatsa. First, a question had to be asked in English, then translated into French, then translated into Hidatsa. The answer had to be translated back from Hidatsa to French to English. Even more translations were needed to understand other native languages such as Shoshone, Arikara, or Assiniboine.

After each question had gone through a two-step translation process, the answer would have to follow the same steps in reverse. For some languages, the translation process would need to go through three or four translations!

1. To appreciate how long a two-step translation process takes, first decode this message using the code below.

Z I V   D V   M L G   W I Z D M   L M D Z I W,   D V

___ ___ ___   ___ ___   ___ ___ ___   ___ ___ ___ ___ ___   ___ ___ ___ ___ ___ ___,   ___ ___

U V D,   W I Z D M   L M D Z I W   G L   M V D   V I Z?

___ ___ ___,   ___ ___ ___ ___ ___   ___ ___ ___ ___ ___ ___   ___ ___   ___ ___ ___   ___ ___ ___?

Hint: Use the opposite letter

A B C D E F G H I J K L M N O P Q R S T U V W X Y Z
Z Y X W V U T S R Q P O N M L K J I H G F E D C B A

2. For the second step, write the message that you decoded *backwards* on the lines below.

___ ___ ___   ___ ___   ___ ___ ___   ___ ___ ___ ___ ___   ___ ___ ___ ___ ___ ___,   ___ ___

___ ___ ___,   ___ ___ ___ ___ ___   ___ ___ ___ ___ ___ ___   ___ ___   ___ ___ ___   ___ ___ ___?

Name: _____ Date: _____

Words to Know

Use a dictionary. Write a definition for each of the following words.

1. Hazardous _____
   _____

2. Obstacle _____
   _____

3. Magpie _____
   _____

4. Portage _____
   _____

5. Capsized _____
   _____

6. Interpreter _____
   _____

7. Dugout _____
   _____

8. Prickly pear _____
   _____

9. Cache _____
   _____

In the space below, draw a scene that illustrates at least four of the words.

Date: _____

Sacajawea

Read the paragraphs about how Sacajawea helped guide the Lewis and Clark expedition. Next, think about someone—perhaps a parent, a teacher, or a coach—who has helped guide you in some way. Finally, answer the questions below.

Touissant Charbonneau was a French Canadian fur trader and interpreter. He was living among the Hidatsa tribe when Lewis and Clark first arrived at the Mandan villages. His young wife, Sacajawea, was a Shoshone native who had been captured by the Hidatsa. Her son, Jean Baptiste, was born in the spring. She called the baby "Pomp," which was Shoshone for "first born."

When the expedition left Fort Mandan, Charbonneau, Sacajawea, and Pomp traveled with them. Sacajawea helped gather native plants and saved valuable supplies from the river when some of the boats almost capsized. Later, she acted as the interpreter to bargain for horses from the Shoshone. Her presence with the expedition also assured native tribes that the Corps of Discovery was not a war party. The tribes all knew that a woman with a child would never accompany a war party.

1. Who has served as your guide? _____

   _____

2. What did the person do to help you? _____

   _____

3. What did you learn from working with this person? _____

   _____

4. What did you learn about yourself in the process? _____

   _____

5. Do you think it's important for young people to have a guide? _____

   _____

6. How could you be a guide for someone else? _____

   _____

Name: _____   Date: _____

A Shipment for President Jefferson

Before the expedition left Fort Mandan, Lewis and Clark prepared a shipment for President Jefferson. Read the list of items they sent Jefferson.

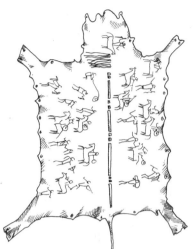

The men packed the keelboat and a canoe with the following items: a live prairie dog, a grouse, and five magpies; a 45-foot skeleton of an ancient reptile; seeds; Native American pottery; soil samples; plant samples; buffalo robes; a robe representing a battle between the Sioux and the Mandans; detailed maps; charts of 53 Native American tribes; horns of deer, elk, and mountain ram; skeletons of antelope, wolf, and bear; skins of red fox, antelope, bear, and marten; reports on the rivers and streams; mineral samples; letters to the President; letters to private friends; and reports about the western lands gathered from the Hidatsa.

A number of soldiers that were not part of the permanent party took the keelboat back down the Missouri River to the Mississippi River to the port of New Orleans. From there, the shipment was taken overland to Washington, D.C.

1. Imagine that it is your job to open the crates for President Jefferson and group the items for his review. List each item in the appropriate category below.

Plant and Land-Related Items

_____

_____

_____

_____

_____

Native American Artifacts

_____

_____

_____

_____

_____

Written Materials

_____

_____

_____

_____

_____

Animal-Related Items

_____

_____

_____

_____

_____

Name: _____ Date: _____

News Reporter for a Day

1. Imagine that the first news of the Lewis and Clark expedition has just reached Washington, D.C. You are a newspaper reporter and want to be the first to write an article about this exciting news. Before you start to write your article, however, you need to be sure of your facts. Use the information from the previous pages to fill in the chart below.

Who: _____

_____

_____

What: _____

_____

_____

Where: _____

_____

_____

When: _____

_____

_____

Why: _____

_____

_____

How: _____

_____

_____

2. Now that you have the facts, write an interesting headline for your article.

_____

3. You have the facts. Now write the article on your own paper. Use vivid descriptions, as well as specific names and places in your article. Inform and update the readers of your newspaper with the exciting adventures of the Lewis and Clark Expedition.

Name: _____ Date: _____

Making a Decision

Lewis and Clark had to make an important decision. Read about it in the paragraph below, then answer questions about a decision you have made.

The Corps left Fort Mandan in April 1805 and headed west on the Missouri River. The land beyond Fort Mandan was known only to the Native Americans. By the end of April, the expedition passed the mouth of the Yellowstone River. They were now in present-day Montana. On June 3, 1805, the expedition came to a large fork in the river. They had to make a decision. The soldiers wanted to take the north fork because it seemed muddy like the Missouri River. Lewis and Clark scouted both forks, then decided to take the southern fork because they felt it led to the mountains. Many of the men weren't convinced it was the right way to go; fortunately, the captains had made the right decision.

1. Describe one important decision that you have made.

   _____

2. What were some things that you had to consider before you made your decision?

   _____

   _____

3. How did you go about making your decision? _____

   _____

4. Did you ask anyone for advice? What advice did the person give you?

   _____

   _____

5. Did your decision affect anyone other than yourself? _____

   _____

6. What were the consequences of your decision? _____

   _____

7. Would you make the same decision again? Why or why not? _____

   _____

   _____

Name: _____ Date: _____

The Great Falls

Read the paragraph about Lewis's reaction when he saw the Great Falls. Next, answer the questions below about a place you enjoy. Finally, write a poem about your favorite place.

The Native Americans had told Lewis about the Great Falls. If Lewis could find the falls, it would prove that he was on the right river route. He took several men with him and went ahead to look for the falls. On June 13, 1805, they found the Great Falls. There, the waters of the Missouri fell 50 feet to the foam below. The sight was so impressive that Lewis stayed there for four hours just to watch it. He said it was the "grandest sight he had ever beheld."

Like Lewis, you may have a place where you like to stay for several hours. It might be somewhere in nature such as a park or near a bubbling brook. It might also be a place such as your grandparents' home.

1. Where do you enjoy going? _____

   _____

2. What do you do while you're in that place? _____

   _____

   _____

3. What makes that place feel special to you? _____

   _____

   _____

4. What good memories do you have from the place? _____

   _____

   _____

5. Use your ideas above to write a short poem about your favorite place on your own paper. Your poem can rhyme or be in free verse.

Name: _____ Date: _____

A Bad Day

Read about Lewis's bad day. Next, fill in the web below with ideas about your worst day. Finally, write a paragraph about what happened to you on that day.

   Lewis hiked alone to the end of the falls and decided to camp there for the night. He had just shot a buffalo for his dinner when he discovered that a grizzly bear was 20 steps behind him! His gun was empty. The grizzly lunged after him. Lewis ran into the river and turned to face the bear. For some reason, the bear fled. Lewis loaded his gun and returned for the buffalo only to find a cougar ready to spring at him. He fired at the cougar, which also fled. Then three bulls from the buffalo herd charged right at him. They finally retreated only a hundred yards from him. Lewis had had enough for one day! He decided to leave the buffalo and return to camp near the other men.

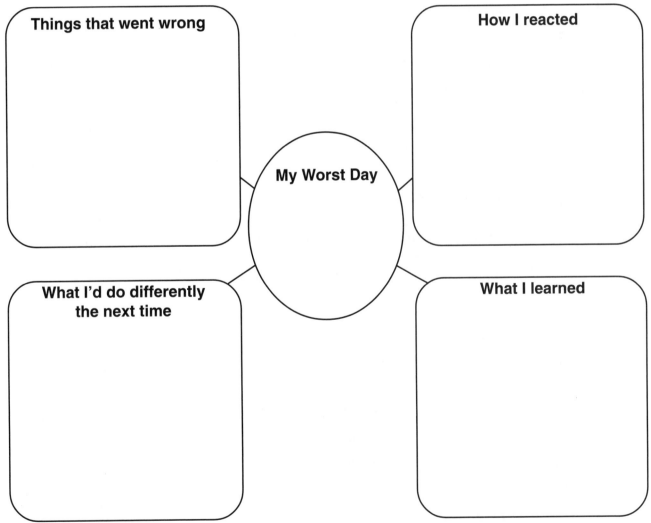

Things that went wrong

How I reacted

My Worst Day

What I'd do differently the next time

What I learned

Use your notes from the web above to write a short paragraph describing your worst day. Write your final copy on your own paper.

Name: _____ Date: _____

The Portage Around the Great Falls

Read the paragraphs and note the order in which events happened.

The Corps of Discovery had to portage almost 20 miles around five falls. They could not take everything with them, so they dug a cache, or hiding place, and put the white pirogue and other supplies into it. They built wagon wheels from a large cottonwood tree and used the mast of the white pirogue to make axles.

The men started the portage on June 22, 1805. They had to make the trip over and over to get the six dugouts and all their supplies around the falls. The men suffered from the heat, gnats, mosquitoes, and prickly pears as they pushed the heavy wagons around the falls. Grizzly bears tried to raid their camp every night, but Lewis's dog, Seaman, managed to keep them away. The men finally finished the portage on the Fourth of July. They celebrated Independence Day by dancing, singing, and telling jokes until late into the evening.

They continued up the Missouri River past the Great Falls. It would soon be cold, and they needed to cross the Rocky Mountains before winter. They needed to find the Shoshone tribe and bargain with them for horses and a guide. The men were tired and bruised; Clark was ill with a fever and had many aches.

At the end of July, the expedition came to three forks in the river. Sacajawea realized that it was the place where the Shoshone tribe had been camped when she was taken away in a raid by the Hidatsa tribe. They knew then that they could not be far from the Shoshone.

Number the events below in the order in which they occurred.

_____ A. They realized that the Shoshone could not be far away.

_____ B. They completed the portage on July 4, 1805.

_____ C. They built a cache and hid the white pirogue and other supplies.

_____ D. They looked for the Shoshone.

_____ E. They started the portage on June 22, 1805.

_____ F. The men suffered from the mosquitoes, gnats, heat, and prickly pears.

_____ G. Sacajawea recognized the three forks in the river.

_____ H. They continued up the Missouri River past the Great Falls.

_____ I. They built wagon wheels from a large cottonwood tree.

_____ J. Clark was ill with a fever and had many aches.

Name: _____ Date: _____

The Name Game

Lewis and Clark had the opportunity to name many places and rivers on their journey. Read the paragraph, and then complete the activity below.

Lewis and Clark named the three forks in the Missouri River the Jefferson, the Madison, and the Gallatin. Madison was the secretary of state, and Gallatin was the secretary of the treasury at the time. They named Fort Mandan to honor the Mandans and the Judith and Marias Rivers in honor of women they liked. They named a stream Floyd's River near the place where Sergeant Floyd had died of appendicitis. They called other rivers the Milk River, Brown Bear Defeated Creek, and Burnt Lodge Creek. They named Slaughter Creek for the place where Native Americans had stampeded a buffalo herd off a cliff. They named Council Bluffs for the place they held the first council with the Native Americans.

Name a river, a park, woods, and a building to honor people you admire or to describe what happened at a place. Finally, write one sentence under each picture explaining why you chose that name.

Name: _____

Why I chose that name: _____

_____

_____

Name: _____

Why I chose that name: _____

_____

_____

Name: _____

Why I chose that name: _____

_____

_____

Name: _____

Why I chose that name: _____

_____

_____

Name: _____ Date: _____

Meeting the Shoshone

Read the paragraphs below and answer the questions.

Lewis and a few men set out from Three Forks in August 1805 to look for the Shoshone tribe. He wanted to bargain with them for horses and a guide across the Rocky Mountains. He was worried because their food supplies were low, and it was hard to find game. The expedition needed to cross the mountains before winter began. The expedition's success and survival depended on finding the Shoshone.

The Shoshone were not well-armed; they feared the Hidatsa and the Blackfeet tribes that lived to the east and northeast. When Lewis finally met several Shoshone, they fled from him in fear. Eventually, he met three Shoshone women. With the help of George Drouillard, the expedition's sign language interpreter, he asked them to take him and his men to the Shoshone camp. They soon encountered 60 Shoshone who, along with their chief, Cameahwait, were going east to hunt buffalo. Lewis convinced them to come with him back to Three Forks to meet Clark and the others who were coming up the river with the canoes. When Sacajawea saw Cameahwait, she realized he was her brother!

Sacajawea had been taken from the Shoshone five years earlier by the Hidatsa tribe. Toussaint Charbonneau, a French Canadian trader, had bought her from the Hidatsa and made her one of his two wives; however, he did not treat her well.

1. If you were Sacajawea, what questions would you want to ask your brother who was now the Shoshone chief? Write two questions below.

_____
_____
_____

2. If you were Cameahwait, what questions would you want to ask your long-lost sister? Write two questions below.

_____
_____
_____

3. If you were Sacajawea, how would you answer the questions?

_____
_____
_____

Name: _____ Date: _____

Adjusting to New Situations

The expedition had to adjust to many new situations. Read each paragraph below and answer the questions.

Lewis and Clark had arrived at the mouth of the Missouri River, 3,000 miles away from where they had started. Lewis still hoped that there would be a branch of the Columbia River nearby, so he sent Clark on ahead to the Shoshone village on the Lemhi River. Clark reported that this river was not navigable. That meant they would have to cross the Rocky Mountains by horse.

Lewis wanted to exchange some of the trade goods for 30 horses. The Shoshone were reluctant to trade unless they received some guns and ammunition. Lewis did not want to part with these items, but he eventually had to exchange some trade goods, a rifle, and a pistol to get the horses.

Thomas Jefferson had thought that it would only be a half-day's portage at most from the Missouri River to a branch of the Columbia River. He thought the Rocky Mountains would be similar to the gentle Appalachian Mountains in the eastern part of the United States. The expedition started out on August 30, 1805, with a Shoshone guide. It took them a week to travel north through the Bitterroot Mountains to the Lolo Trail, which was a native route they would then follow west through the Rocky Mountains. The entire portage took almost a month.

1. What had Lewis hoped for? _____

_____

2. What did the expedition have to do? _____

_____

3. What did Lewis want to trade? _____

_____

4. What did he end up trading? _____

_____

5. How long did Jefferson think it would take to portage from the Missouri River to the Columbia River? _____

6. How long did it take them to make the entire portage? _____

Name: _____ Date: _____

Crossing the Lolo Trail

Read the paragraphs and complete the activity below.

The trip across the Lolo Trail was the most difficult part of the entire expedition. The men had to hack their way through thickets as they traveled on a narrow footpath up and down the stony mountains. The narrow ledge was so steep that horses fell backwards down the trail or off the side. One horse fell 100 yards down into a creek, but amazingly, it was not badly injured.

It rained, and the men ached with cold. One morning they awoke to find themselves covered with snow. Their food supply was low, and the hunters could not find any game. They lived on the portable soup Lewis had brought all the way from Philadelphia. They even ate a few of the colts; however, the men became extremely weak and exhausted. Finally, they saw the prairie 60 miles away.

The men experienced many emotions as they struggled across the Lolo Trail. Choose five words from the word box below that describe the men's feelings as they crossed the Lolo Trail. Use each word in a sentence that explains why the men might have felt that way. An example has been given.

angry	determined	concerned	wise
good-humored	brave	defeated	caring
exhausted	relaxed	excited	distracted

Example: The men were *determined* to get over the Lolo Trail because they did not turn back.

1. _____

   _____

2. _____

   _____

3. _____

   _____

4. _____

   _____

5. _____

   _____

Name: _____ Date: _____

The Continental Divide

The Continental Divide is the highest part of North America. It divides the waters that flow into the Atlantic from those that flow into the Pacific. The Continental Divide is high in the Rocky Mountains. It runs along New Mexico, Colorado, Wyoming, Idaho, and Montana. The Continental Divide also runs through Canada to the north and through Mexico and Central America to the south.

Study the map below, then answer the questions.

1. The rivers east of the Continental Divide flow towards the _____ Ocean.

2. The rivers west of the Continental Divide flow towards the _____ Ocean.

3. When the men left St. Louis, Missouri, and traveled up the Missouri River, were they going with or against the current? _____

4. How did that affect their progress? _____

5. When the men traveled down the Clearwater River, the Snake River, and the Columbia River on their way to the Pacific Ocean, were they going with or against the current?

   _____

6. When the men traveled up the Columbia River on the way back from the Pacific Ocean, were they going with or against the current? _____

7. When the men traveled down the Missouri River on the way back from the Pacific, were they going with or against the current? _____

8. How did that affect their progress? _____

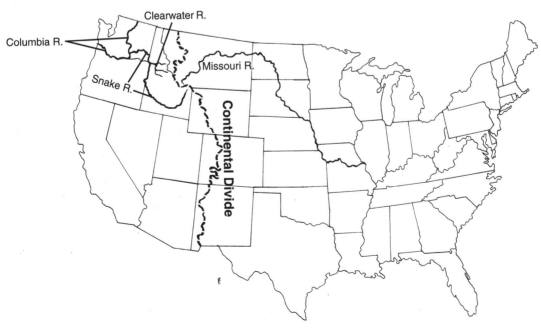

Name: _____ Date: _____

Good News, Bad News

The men had both bad news and good news after they crossed the Lolo Trail. Read the paragraphs, then fill in each section below with the bad news or the good news.

The Corps of Discovery had crossed the Rocky Mountains and made it to a Nez Percé village. The men were so exhausted that they did not have enough strength to hollow out new canoes. They were able to make canoes, however, by using the easier Nez Percé method of burning out logs. After they had rested awhile, the men left the village and headed down the Clearwater River. It was the first time since the expedition left St. Louis that they had traveled with the current. Although they traveled downstream, the river had many dangerous rapids. On the first day, one canoe hit a rock and began to take on water. Some of the men couldn't swim, so they clung to the submerged canoe in the middle of the river. Fortunately, the other men came to their rescue.

The expedition was able to make 30 to 40 miles a day in spite of the fact that they often had to stop to portage around rapids or to dry their supplies. They also lost supplies and trade goods while running the rapids. There wasn't much game in the area, but there were many Native American villages where the men could stop each day to buy dog meat and fish. Unfortunately, many villages were infested by fleas.

1. **Bad News:** The men were too tired to hollow out new canoes.
    Good News: _____
    _____

2. **Good News:** The men traveled with the current.
    Bad News: _____
    _____

3. **Bad News:** The canoe hit a rock and took on water. Some of the men couldn't swim.
    Good News: _____
    _____

4. **Good News:** The men traveled 30 to 40 miles a day.
    Bad News: _____
    _____

5. **Good News:** There were many Native American villages where the men could stop
    each day to buy dog meat and fish.
    Bad News: _____
    _____

Name: _____ Date: _____

Pacific Ahead!

Read the paragraphs about the expedition's travel down the Columbia River to the Pacific Ocean, and complete the activity that follows.

The expedition continued down the Clearwater River to the Snake River. The Corps of Discovery met many natives along the way, including the friendly Walla Wallas. On October 16, 1805, they traveled onto a larger river, the Columbia. This river was the biggest river they had seen on their journey. It was also the hardest one to navigate because of the long stretches of rapids. The weather on the upper Columbia was dry, but when the men reached the lower Columbia, the weather became cloudy, foggy, and damp, and it rained continuously.

The Columbia River started to rise and fall with the ocean tides. The men saw seagulls and other seabirds. They also saw natives with trade goods obtained from the trading ships that visited the Pacific coast in search of sea otter pelts. Some natives were wearing sailors' jackets and hats. They even met natives who knew some English words.

On November 7, 1805, William Clark wrote in his journal, "Ocean in view, O! the joy!" In fact, it was not yet the ocean. It was a wide part of the river now known as Gray's Bay, 20 miles from the ocean. By November 15, the men could no longer travel on the river because the waves were too high. They spent several soggy weeks camped near the mouth of the Columbia River with the ocean in view. The rain started to rot their leather clothes and their supplies. Everything was wet; nothing ever dried. Lewis took some men ahead by land to look for any sign of ships on the coast; there were none. Later, Clark took the others to see the ocean. The men were so soaked by rain that they only wanted to head back upstream and find a dry campsite where they could wait out the winter.

Read the statements below and decide if each one is true or false. Write "T" for true and "F" for false.

_____ 1. The men experienced pleasant weather all the way down the Columbia River.

_____ 2. The Clearwater River runs into the Snake River.

_____ 3. The Columbia River did not contain many rapids.

_____ 4. The Snake River rose and fell with the tides.

_____ 5. The men saw trading ships on the Pacific Ocean.

_____ 6. Some natives knew some English words.

_____ 7. The men were more interested in finding a dry campsite than in seeing the Pacific Ocean.

_____ 8. Trade ships that traveled along the Pacific coast were in search of sea otter pelts.

_____ 9. The mouth of the Columbia River is near the Pacific Ocean.

_____ 10. The men planned to return to St. Louis before winter completely set in.

47

Name: _____   Date: _____

Interviewing Lewis, Clark, and Sacajawea

Imagine that you are on a trade ship that has stopped near the mouth of the Columbia River. You had heard about the expedition, and now, to your surprise, you actually meet Lewis, Clark, and Sacajawea near the Pacific Ocean. You are the first person to interview them. Write three questions each for Captain Lewis, Captain Clark, and Sacajawea.

Questions for Captain Lewis:

1. _____
   _____
2. _____
   _____
3. _____
   _____

Lewis

Questions for Captain Clark:

1. _____
   _____
2. _____
   _____
3. _____
   _____

Clark

Questions for Sacajawea:

1. _____
   _____
2. _____
   _____
3. _____
   _____

Sacajawea

Use your own paper to answer the questions the way you think Lewis, Clark, and Sacajawea would have responded.

Name: _____   Date: _____

Reviewing the Journey: Part 3

The paragraph below reviews the route the Corps of Discovery followed. Read the paragraph and do the mapping activity below.

The Corps of Discovery had traveled west on the Missouri River from Fort Mandan. They took the southern fork of the Missouri River past Great Falls to Three Forks. They followed the westernmost fork that they named the Jefferson River for a ways. From there, they traveled north by land through the Bitterroot Range of the Rocky Mountains to the Lolo Trail. Then they went west on the Lolo Trail through the Rocky Mountains. They traveled from the Clearwater River, to the Snake River, to the Columbia River, to the Pacific Ocean. They spent the winter at Fort Clatsop.

1. Use reference books to label the following rivers and states on the map below:
    • Missouri River, Jefferson River, Clearwater River, Snake River, Columbia River
    • North Dakota, Montana, Idaho, Washington, Oregon

2. Label Great Falls, Three Forks, the Bitterroot Range, the Lolo Trail, and Fort Clatsop.

3. Use a red pencil to indicate the route the expedition took from the Mandan villages to the Pacific Ocean.

49

Name: _____   Date: _____

Winter at Fort Clatsop

Read the paragraph about the expedition's stay at Fort Clatsop and write an entry in Lewis's journal. Include information under three categories: *Our Horrible Diet, Our Problems,* and *Our Accomplishments.*

    The men could not stay beside the mouth of the Columbia River because of the bad weather and the lack of food. They did not have enough trade goods to buy food from the natives. They traveled back up the Columbia to an area where they built Fort Clatsop, named in honor of a local tribe. There the men hunted elk and dug for roots. They boiled salt water, extracted the salt, and used it to season the lean, stringy elk and the roots. The winter was long and monotonous, and it rained continuously. The men were both sick and homesick. They could not get rid of the fleas. Still, the men used the time to make 368 pairs of elk moccasins, new shirts, and pants. Clark worked on a detailed map. He knew now that they had gone six hundred miles out of their way and figured out how to make a shorter return trip. Everyone still hoped that they could return with a passing trade ship.

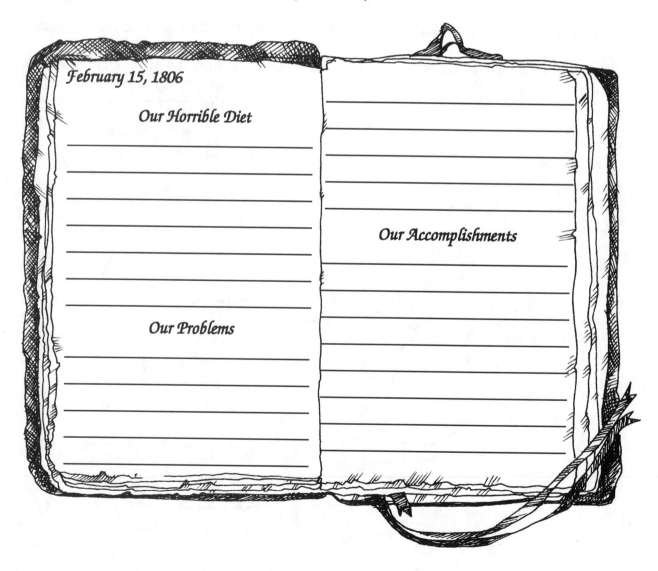

February 15, 1806

Our Horrible Diet

Our Problems

Our Accomplishments

Name: _____ Date: _____

The Journey Home

Read the paragraphs about the journey home and answer the questions below.

The expedition left Fort Clatsop on March 23, 1806. The Corps of Discovery headed up the Columbia River, but this time they had to travel against the current. By May 3, the expedition had reached the Nez Percé villages where they retrieved the horses they had left there the previous winter. With the help of several Nez Percé guides, they crossed the Lolo Trail in only six days.

From there, Lewis went north to explore the Marias River. He wanted to see if this river would be a water route up to Canada and its rich fur trade. The river, however, veered into the Rockies. After that, he had a serious clash with the Blackfeet tribe. Later, Lewis and his men were hunting elk when one of the men accidentally shot Lewis in the behind.

Clark's team took a different route. They went past Three Forks, then down the Yellowstone River to the Missouri. There his team met up with Lewis's team. The Mandan Chief Sheheke joined the explorers so he could visit President Jefferson. They returned to St. Louis by September 21, 1806; the journey home had only taken them six months.

1. Why was the journey home from the Pacific so much faster than the journey going to the Pacific? _____

_____

_____

2. What experience did the men gain on the way to the Pacific that they used on the way home? _____

_____

_____

3. What landmarks did the men use on the way home that they did not have on the way there? _____

_____

_____

4. What landmarks do you use to help you "navigate" around your city or town?

_____

_____

Name: _____ Date: _____

The Arrival Home

Can you imagine some of the conversations that took place between the men and the people in St. Louis? Read the paragraph, then fill in the boxes below with conversations that might have taken place between the townspeople and Lewis and Clark.

As the expedition neared home, the men cheered when they saw cows on the riverbank. A few days later, they learned from some traders that they had been given up for dead long ago. They stopped first in St. Charles and were met by the excited townspeople. They continued down the Missouri to St. Louis, where they were welcomed home by the whole town. One newspaper's account described them as "Robinson Crusoes—dressed entirely in buckskins."

Meriwether Lewis

William Clark

Name: _____ Date: _____

Souvenirs

People often purchase or collect souvenirs when they go on a vacation. For example, some people might buy a T-shirt with the name of the place they are visiting. Others might draw a picture of a sight they want to remember. Still others might collect a seashell from a beach or a leaf from a tree as a souvenir.

1. If you had been on the expedition with Lewis and Clark, what kinds of souvenirs would you have brought back for yourself or your family? List five ideas below.

   _____

   _____

   _____

   _____

2. Select one of your ideas above. Explain why you selected that souvenir. Why is it important to you? What do you plan to do with it? Where did you collect it?

   _____

   _____

   _____

3. Draw a picture of the souvenir below.

Name: _____ Date: _____

Mission Accomplished

Use what you learned in this book to judge whether the Lewis and Clark expedition accomplished its mission. Fill in the chart below. Place a check in the appropriate column for each goal.

The Goals of the Mission	Goal Met	Goal Not Met	Goal Only Partially Met
1. Draw accurate maps.			
2. Record information about climate, soil, plants, and animals.			
3. Keep a detailed journal.			
4. Make friends with the Native Americans.			
5. Find out about the Native Americans' cultures.			
6. Find a water route to the Pacific Ocean.			

7. Which goal was not met? Explain why.

_____

_____

_____

8. Which goal was only partially met? Explain why.

_____

_____

_____

9. How would you rate the overall success of the expedition using the scale below? Circle the number you think represents the degree of success of the expedition.

0   1   2   3   4   5   6   7   8   9   10

Unsuccessful   Partially Successful   Totally Successful

54

Name: _____ Date: _____

After the Expedition

Lewis arrived in Washington, D.C., in December, 1806, and Clark in January of 1807.

After the expedition, the privates and the sergeants received their pay. To reward a job well done, each one was given double pay. For the privates, that amounted to ten dollars per month. The sergeants received 16 dollars per month. Since the expedition had been gone 28 months, how much money did the privates receive? How much did the sergeants receive?

Each man also received 320 acres of land. He also had the choice to remain in the army and pick his next place of duty or to receive an honorable discharge.

York received his freedom from William Clark. He returned to Louisville, Kentucky, and went into the freight-hauling business.

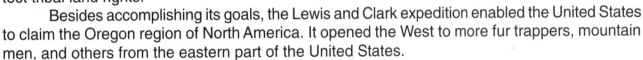

Charbonneau, who had been a civilian translator for the expedition, received $500 for his work although he was, according to Lewis, "a man of no particular merit." He stayed at the Mandan villages with Sacajawea and Pomp. Pomp later went east, and Clark paid for his education. Sacajawea may have died in 1812. Some people believed she lived among the Shoshone in the Wind River Mountains of Wyoming until she was 94 years old.

Each captain received 1,600 acres of land and $1,228. Lewis became the Governor of the Upper Louisiana Territory. Clark became the Superintendent of Indian Affairs. He worked to protect tribal land rights.

Besides accomplishing its goals, the Lewis and Clark expedition enabled the United States to claim the Oregon region of North America. It opened the West to more fur trappers, mountain men, and others from the eastern part of the United States.

1. How do you think Lewis and Clark were received by Jefferson and by the public?

   _____

   _____

2. What was the total amount paid to the privates? _____

3. What was the total amount paid to the sergeants? _____

4. Do you think granting his freedom was a good way to compensate York? Why or why not?

   _____

   _____

5. Do you think Sacajawea should have been paid for her work? Why or why not?

   _____

   _____

Name: _____ Date: _____

Life Lessons

1. When Lewis was young, his father taught him the family motto: "To the brave man, everything he does is for his country." How did this motto influence Lewis?

   _____

   _____

2. There are many kinds of family mottoes. For example, one family's motto might be *Clean up after yourself.* Another family's motto might be *Treat the earth with respect.* Think about the ideas that are important to your family. Write a motto that is appropriate for your family.

   _____

3. How do you think that motto influences your family? _____

   _____

   _____

4. How do you predict that motto will affect you in the future? _____

   _____

   _____

5. Lewis's mother taught him important lessons about loyalty and obedience. From what you have learned about Lewis, give an example of a time when he was:

   a. loyal _____

   b. obedient _____

6. What important lessons have you learned from your parents? _____

   _____

   _____

7. Give examples of how you have demonstrated those lessons. _____

   _____

   _____

   _____

8. What lessons do you want your future children to learn? Why? _____

   _____

   _____

   _____

Name: _____ Date: _____

Designing a Stamp

What kind of a stamp would you design to honor the Lewis and Clark expedition? You could draw a picture of one of the animals they encountered, such as a grizzly bear, a prairie dog, or a magpie. You could draw a picture of their starting point at Camp Wood on the Missouri River. You could draw a picture of Sacajawea with her infant son, Jean Baptiste. List five of your ideas below.

1. _____
2. _____
3. _____
4. _____
5. _____

After you decide what to draw, use reference books to help you design a picture that is accurate, detailed, and colorful. Draw the picture in the stamp below. Add a postage amount of your choice.

THE LEWIS AND CLARK EXPEDITION
1804–1806

Name: _____   Date: _____

Trivia Quiz

How much do you remember about the Lewis and Clark expedition? Complete the trivia quiz below.

1. Who was Thomas Jefferson's personal secretary in 1801? _____

2. From whom did the United States purchase the Louisiana Territory? _____

3. In what year did the United States purchase the Louisiana Territory? _____

4. How much did the United States pay for the purchase? _____

5. President Jefferson wanted Lewis and Clark to find a _____ route to the Pacific.

6. The Missouri River joins the _____ River at St. Louis, Missouri.

7. In what year did the Lewis and Clark expedition leave St. Louis? _____

8. What was York's heritage? _____

9. Pierre Cruzatte played the _____.

10. John Shields was a skilled gunsmith and _____.

11. What is the Missouri River's nickname? _____

12. Which captain was the better riverboatman? _____

13. Which captain was the better naturalist? _____

14. In the summer, the Otos and Missouri tribes hunted _____.

15. What name did Lewis and Clark give to the place where they had the first council with the Native Americans? _____

16. Which group of Native Americans tried to control trading between fur traders and the tribes north of them on the Missouri River? _____

17. Which tribe let the expedition winter near them in 1804? _____

18. Fort Mandan was located near present-day _____, North Dakota.

19. What was the name of Sacajawea's son? _____

20. The portage around _____ took almost a month.

21. The Missouri branched into three rivers at Three Forks. The names of the three rivers were _____, _____, and _____.

22. The expedition needed to obtain _____ and a guide from the Shoshone.

23. Who was Sacajawea's brother? _____

24. The expedition crossed the _____ Trail over the Rocky Mountains.

25. The rivers east of the Continental Divide flow to the _____ Ocean.

26. The Clearwater River runs into the _____ River.

27. The Snake River runs into the _____ River.

28. Give the name of the fort near the mouth of the Columbia River. _____

29. On the way home, Lewis had a serious clash with the _____ tribe.

30. In what year did the expedition arrive back in St. Louis? _____

Name: _____   Date: _____

Searching for Lewis and Clark

Find and circle these 32 words in the word search puzzle below. Words are printed forward, backward, horizontally, vertically, and diagonally in the puzzle.

Lewis	Corps	York	Sacajawea	expedition	Clark
Pomp	keelboat	Missouri	pirogue	portage	Mandan
Columbia	Jefferson	buffalo	horses	natives	river
Walla Wallas	plains	Snake	Chinook	Blackfeet	dugout
Shoshone	trade	Sioux	grizzly	Nez Percé	Yakima
Seaman	boats				

```
M W X I Z Q P P W F T U O G U D K Q M S
N K N R K J G N E Z P E R C E G A O T E
O O A U N R Y A K I M A S Z K Y F A A L
I O I O A R O P Q C A S W Y E L O S P T
T N K S T O Y Y G D O W Q E P B O A I N
I I E S I A L X T H I L B L A Y Z Q R O
D H E I V E G A N O O X U Q R J Y S O S
E C L M E W Z Y F O X R F M Q C V H G R
P C B C S A L E S F Z U S R B H H O U E
X G O P N J D S S B U Q O E I I D S E F
E B A K W A R A X I E B I I S L A H R F
Y L T Q R C I L W D W U D F S Q Q O T E
L A J T R A V L V A T E P M O P N N B J
Z C M N P S O A O N H D L L L M C E L S
Z K C H O U Y W N A M A E S R O B M F N
I F Q S R R D A E D L H Y E R G E I C I
R E J W T C R L E N Q Z V P E P K L L A
G E D N A X Q L X A N I S A V O A M B L
S T R G G L V A K M R R B A V R N Z H P
W I F V E G N W N H X E B F K K S R C E
```

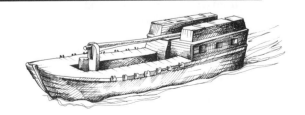

Answer Keys

Meet Meriwether Lewis (p. 3)
1. His father left home to fight against the British.
2. There were no schools in Georgia.
3. Lewis was interested in plants.
4. He attended school.
5. He enjoyed his experience in the militia.
6. He became a friend of William Clark.

Meet William Clark (p. 4)
1. August 1, 1770; near Richmond, Virginia
2. Virginia to Kentucky
3. Natural history and science
4. Hunting, fishing, tracking, camping, land navigation
5. Captain
6. Respected the Native Americans

Important Words to Learn (p. 5)
1. Botany - the scientific study of plants
2. Zoology - the science that deals with the study of animal life
3. Naturalist - someone who studies animals and plants
4. Herb - a plant used in cooking or medicine
5. Celestial - to do with the sky
6. Navigate - to travel in a ship, an aircraft, or other vehicle using maps, compasses, the stars, etc., to guide you
7. Expedition - a long journey for a special purpose, such as exploring

Comparing and Contrasting Lewis and Clark (p. 6)
Lewis Only: five years of formal schooling; naturalist; studied medicine, botany, zoology, and celestial navigation; slender build; dark hair; moody and impatient
Clark Only: no formal schooling; geographer; mapmaker; nature artist; riverboatman; skilled in trapping and camping; stocky build; red hair; sociable and even-tempered
Both Lewis and Clark: born in Virginia; skilled in hunting and fishing; over six feet tall; captains in the army

The Louisiana Purchase (p. 8)
1. Louisiana, Arkansas, Missouri, Iowa, Minnesota, North Dakota, South Dakota, Nebraska, Kansas, Oklahoma, Texas, New Mexico, Colorado, Wyoming, Montana (Source maps will differ.)

The Oregon Country (p. 9)
1. Montana, Idaho, Washington, Oregon

Getting Your Bearings (p. 12)
1. Latitude - the position of a place, measured in degrees north or south of the equator
2. Longitude - the position of a place, measured in degrees east or west of a line that runs through the Greenwich Observatory in London, England; on a map or globe, lines of longitude are drawn from the North Pole to the South Pole
3. Sextant - an instrument for measuring angular distances used especially in navigation to observe altitudes of celestial bodies (as in ascertaining latitude and longitude)

4. Octant - an instrument for observing altitudes of a celestial body from a moving ship or aircraft.
5. Philadelphia, Pennsylvania: 40°N 75°W
6. Louisville, Kentucky: 38°N 86°W
7. St. Louis, Missouri: 38°N 90°W
8. Bismarck, North Dakota: 47°N 101°W
9. Council Bluffs, Iowa: 41°N 96°W
10. Astoria, Oregon: 46°N 124°W

Problems and Solutions (p. 18)
1. Problem: It was too late to continue because the Missouri River froze in winter.
   Solution: They built Fort Wood and stayed there until spring.
2. Problem: Many of the men did not know how to shoot a rifle correctly.
   Solution: They underwent constant rifle practice.
3. Problem: Some men refused to obey orders.
   Solution: Those men were dismissed.
4. Problem: President Jefferson wanted to be informed about the expedition's progress.
   Solution: Some men would stay with the expedition only for a while, then they would return with reports and artifacts for Jefferson.

Reviewing the Journey: Part 1 (p. 19)
Teacher check map.

The Keelboat and the Pirogues (p. 21)
1. Keelboat - a large, shallow freight boat with a keel (a timber that extends the entire length of the bottom of the boat)
   Pirogue - a dugout canoe; a canoe-shaped boat
2. French

The Muddy Missouri (p. 22)
Actual Information:
1. Four parts water, six parts mud and sand
2. They could pole or tow the boats around sandbars.
3. There were boulders and rapids. They were going against the current.
4. About 12 to 14 miles a day

The First Council With the Native Americans (p. 26)
Neither side got what it wanted because both sides had completely different goals.

Now and Then (p. 27)
Only the crew of the expedition:
Trade blacksmith services for corn; hunt buffalo; row a keelboat
Only people today:
Watch a movie; use a computer; play baseball
Both men on the expedition and people today:
Go for a swim; dance, sing, listen to music; play checkers; observe plants and animals; read a book; write letters; take a nature walk; swat mosquitoes; converse in sign language; write in a journal; gather berries; eat soup

60

The Teton Sioux (p. 28)
A. 4; B. 10; C. 1; D. 3; E. 2; F. 6; G. 9; H. 5; I. 7; J. 8

Winter at Fort Mandan (p. 29)
Mandans: played lacrosse on the frozen river while wearing very few clothes; gave the men corn for the blacksmith services; hunted for buffalo; visited the blacksmith shop and examined the keelboat

The Corps of Discovery: struggled to stay warm; set up a blacksmith shop where they sharpened and repaired axes, hoes, and other metal tools for the Mandans; hunted for buffalo; visited the Mandan village and danced for the Mandans; Lewis and Clark spent the winter writing detailed reports and making accurate maps for President Jefferson.

Reviewing the Journey Part 2 (p. 30)
A. Bismarck, North Dakota
B. Sioux City, Iowa
C. Council Bluffs, Iowa
D. Kansas City, Missouri
E. St. Louis, Missouri

In Mathematical Terms (p. 31)
1. Clark, four years
2. They were too young.
3. Lewis was 29. Clark was 33. (The expedition left in May. Their birthdays were in August.)
4. 17 years
5. 1,000 miles
6. 7,000 pounds
7. $10
8. $5
9. 2,000
10. 72 years

From One Language to Another (p. 32)
1. Are we not drawn onward, we few, drawn onward to new era?
2. Are we not drawn onward, we few, drawn onward to new era? (Palindrome)

Words to Know (p. 33)
1. Hazardous - dangerous or risky
2. Obstacle - something that gets in your way or prevents you from doing something
3. Magpie - a noisy, black and white bird with a large beak and long tail feathers
4. Portage - to carry a boat or goods from one body of water to another
5. Capsized - overturned or upset, especially a boat in the water
6. Interpreter - a person who translates from one language to another
7. Dugout - a canoe made from the outer portion of a large log
8. Prickly pear - a cactus with yellow flowers and fruit shaped like a pear
9. Cache - a hiding place, especially for concealing and preserving supplies

A Shipment for President Jefferson (p. 35)
Plant and Land-Related Items:
   Seeds; soil samples; plant samples; mineral samples
Native American Artifacts:
   Native American pottery; buffalo robes; a robe representing a battle between the Sioux and the Mandans
Written Materials:
   detailed maps; charts of 53 Native American tribes; letters to the President; letters to private friends; reports about the western lands gathered from the Hidatsa; reports on the rivers and streams
Animal-Related Items:
   a live prairie dog, a grouse, and five magpies; a 45-foot skeleton of an ancient reptile; horns of deer, elk, and mountain ram; skeletons of antelope, wolf, and bear; skins of red fox, antelope, bear, and marten

The Portage around the Great Falls (p. 40)
A. 10; B. 5; C. 1; D. 7; E. 3; F. 4; G. 9; H. 6; I. 2; J. 8

Adjusting to New Situations (p. 43)
1. Lewis hoped to find a branch of the Columbia River nearby.
2. They had to cross the Rocky Mountains by horse instead.
3. Lewis wanted to exchange trade goods for 30 horses.
4. He had to exchange trade goods plus a rifle and a pistol to get the horses.
5. Jefferson thought it would take one-half day to portage from the Missouri to the Columbia River.
6. It took almost a month to cross the Rocky Mountains and make the portage.

The Continental Divide (p. 45)
1. Atlantic   2. Pacific
3. Against   4. It slowed them down.
5. With   6. Against
7. With   8. It helped them go faster.

Good News, Bad News (p. 46)
1. They used the Nez Percé method of burning out logs to make canoes.
2. The river was full of dangerous rapids.
3. The other men rescued them.
4. They often had to stop to portage around rapids or dry their supplies.
5. The villages were infested with fleas.

Pacific Ahead! (p. 47)
1. F; 2. T; 3. F; 4. F; 5. F; 6. T; 7. T; 8. T; 9. T; 10. F

Reviewing the Journey: Part 3 (p. 49)
Teacher check map.

The Journey Home (p. 51)
1. They traveled with the current and knew where they were going.
2. They had learned how to handle the boats, when to portage over the rapids, how to interact with the natives, and how to hunt efficiently.
3. The Nez Percé village, the Lolo Trail, Three Forks, Great Falls, the Mandan Villages, Council Bluffs, Platte River, etc.

Mission Accomplished (p. 54)
1. met
2. met
3. met
4. partially met
5. met
6. not met
7. They did not find a water route to the west because they had to go over the Rocky Mountains by horse.
8. They were able to make friends with some, but not all the tribes.
9. Student decision

After the Expedition (p. 55)
1. They were considered heroes.
2. $280
3. $448

Trivia Quiz (p. 58)
1. Meriwether Lewis
2. France
3. 1803
4. $15 million
5. water
6. Mississippi
7. 1804
8. African-American
9. fiddle or violin
10. blacksmith
11. The Big Muddy
12. Clark
13. Lewis
14. buffalo
15. Council Bluffs

16. Teton Sioux
17. Mandans
18. Bismarck
19. Jean Baptiste or Pomp
20. Great Falls
21. Jefferson, Gallatin, and Madison
22. horses
23. Cameahwait
24. Lolo
25. Atlantic
26. Snake
27. Columbia
28. Clatsop
29. Blackfeet
30. 1806

Searching for Lewis and Clark (p. 59)

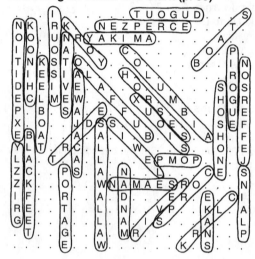

Suggested Reading

Andrist, Ralph K. *To the Pacific with Lewis and Clark.* New York: American Heritage Publishing Co., Inc. (1967)

Bowen, Andy Russel. *The Back of Beyond: A Story about Lewis and Clark.* Minneapolis, Minnesota: Carolrhoda Books, Inc. (1997)

Cavan, Seamus. *Lewis and Clark and the Route to the Pacific.* New York: Chelsea House Publishers. (1991)

Fitzgerald, Christine A. *The World's Greatest Explorers: Meriwether Lewis and William Clark.* Chicago: Children's Press. (1991)

Morley, Jacqueline. *Across America: The Story of Lewis and Clark.* New York: Franklin Watts. (1998)

Petersen, David and Mark Coburn. *Meriwether Lewis and William Clark: Soldiers, Explorers, and Partners in History.* Chicago: Children's Press. (1988)

Schanzer, Rosalyn. *How We Crossed the West: The Adventures of Lewis and Clark.* Washington, D.C.: National Geographic Society. (1997)

Stein, R. Conrad. *The Story of the Lewis and Clark Expedition.* Chicago: Children's Press. (1978)

Thorp, Daniel B. *Lewis and Clark: An American Journey.* New York: Metro Books. (1998)